しんわのえほん
神話の絵本
Japanese Mythology
Picture Book

出雲 Izumo
出雲国 (いずものくに) Izumo's country
因幡 Inaba

瀬戸内海 (せとないかい) Seto Inland Sea

浪速 (なにわ) Naniwa
大和国 (やまとのくに) Yamato's country
橿原 (かしはら) Kashihara
宇陀 (うだ) Uda
吉野 (よしの) Yoshino
紀伊 (きい) Kii
熊野 (くまの) Kumano

日向国 (ひむかのくに) Himuka's country
美々津 (みみつ) Mimitsu
阿波岐原 (あわさはら) Awakihara
高千穂の宮 (たかちほのみや) Takachihonomiya

第一幕 高天原(たかまのはら)神話

第1章 国生み神生み

何もない宇宙に、天と地ができました。
天の高天原に男の神イザナキと
女の神イザナミが生まれました。
その頃地上はまだ泥沼のようでした。
二人は日本の国土を生みました。
これを国生みと言います。
次に彼らは自然の神を生みました。
すなわち、海の神、川の神、
山の神、木の神、草の神などです。
これを神生みと言います。

「高天原」は、天のどこかにある、
想像上の、野原のことです。
「イザナキ」と「イザナミ」は「いざなう」を意味します。
「いざなう」は、「お互いに誘い合う」を意味します。
それは「男と女が誘い合う」を意味します。

ACT I *Takamanohara* Mythology

Chapter 1. *KuniUmi & KamiUmi*
(means the creation of lands and gods)

The heaven and land were created
in the empty universe.
A male god *Izanaki* and
a female god *Izanami* were born
in the *Takamanohara* heaven.
At that time, the ground was like a swamp.
The couple created the lands of Japan.
This is called *Kuniumi*.
Next, they created the gods of nature.
They are the gods of the seas, rivers,
mountains, trees, grasses, etc.
This is called *Kamiumi*.

Takamanohara is an imaginary field
somewhere in the heaven.
Izanaki and *Izanami* means *Izanau*.
Izanau means to invite each other.
It means Man and Woman invite each other.

ACT 幕
mythology 神話

Chapter 章
mean 意味する
creation 生み
land 国土
gods 神々

heaven 天
land 地
create できた
empty 何もない
universe 宇宙
male 男の
female 女の
bear-bore-born
　　　　　生まれた

At that time その頃
ground 地上
like 〜のよう
swamp 泥沼
couple ふたり
call 言います
next 次に
nature 自然
sea 海
river 川
mountain 山
tree 木
grass 草
etc など(etcetera)

imaginary 想像上の
field 野原
somewhere どこか
invite 誘い合う
each other お互いに

The heaven and land were created in the empty universe.
A male god *Izanaki* and a female god *Izanami* were born in the *Takamanohara* heaven.

At that time, the ground was like a swamp. The couple created the lands of Japan. This is called *Kuniumi*.

Next, they created the gods of nature. They are the gods of the seas, rivers, mountains, trees, grasses, etc. This is called *Kamiumi*.

第2章 禊ぎ

イザナミは、神生みの最後に、
燃える火の神を産んだとき、
火傷で死んでしまいました。
イザナキは、妻のイザナミを追って、
地下にある、死の国・黄泉の国へ
行きました。
しかし、彼は妻の変わり果てた
恐ろしい姿を見て、
穢れを受け、
地上へ逃げ帰りました。
彼は日向の阿波岐原で
穢れを落としました。
すなわち、彼は体を清めるために、
儀式の禊ぎをしました。

「日向」は、古い地名で、
現在の「宮崎県」です。
「阿波岐原」は、地名で、
宮崎市にあります。

Chapter 2. *Misogi*
(it means the "purification ceremony".)

At the end of *Kamiumi*,
after *Izanami* gave birth to
the Fire god, she died of burns.
Izanaki followed his wife *Izanami*
to the country of the dead, *Yomi*,
located underground.
However, he saw his wife's changing
and horrible appearance,
receiving *Kegare*,
he returned to the ground.
He dropped his *Kegare*
at *Himuka*'s *Awakihara*.
That is, he performed the *Misogi*
ceremony to purify his body.

Himuka is the old place name,
of current *Miyazaki prefecture*.
Awakihara is the place name,
and is in *Miyazaki* city.

---

purification 清め
ceremony 儀式

end 最後
give birth 生む
fire's god 火の神
die 死ぬ
burns ヤケド
follow 追って行く
wife 妻
country 国
dead 死
locat ～にある
underground 地下

however しかし
changing 変わり果て
horrible 恐ろしい
appearance 姿
receive 受ける
return 逃げ帰る
ground 地上
drop 落とす
that is すなわち
perform 行う
ceremony 儀式
purify 清める
body 体

place-name 地名
current 現在の
prefecture 県
city 市

第3章 天照 誕生

イザナキが禊ぎをしたときに、
アマテラスは、左目から生まれました。
スサノオは、鼻から生まれました。
その後、アマテラスは、天の高天原
を治めました。
しかしスサノオは泣いてばかりでした。
それで、父のイザナキから叱られ、
そして、追放されました。
それで、彼は姉さんのアマテラスに
別れの挨拶をするため
天へ登ってゆきました。
しかし、彼女は彼を疑いました。
彼女は言った、「彼は、この天を、
乗っ取りに来たに違いない。」
それで、彼女は、戦闘服姿で、
待ち構えました。

「アマテラス」は、日本の皇室の祖先の神様です。
「天」は、天を意味し、「照」には、照らすを意味します。
それで、彼女は、太陽の神です。

Chapter 3. Amaterasu's Birth

When *Izanaki* performed *Misogi*,
Amaterasu was born from his left eye,
and *Susanoo* was born from his nose.
After that, *Amaterasu* ruled
the heaven *Takamanohara*.
But, *Susanoo* did nothing but cry.
So, he was scolded and kicked out
by his father *Izanaki*.
So, he climbed to the heaven
to say good-bye
to his older sister *Amaterasu*.
However, she was suspicious of him.
She thought "He must have come to
take over this heaven".
So, she was waiting for him
in her combat uniform.

Amaterasu is the god of the
japanese empire's ancestor.
Ama means heaven, *Terasu* means light up,
So, she is the god of the sun.

---

birth 誕生

perform 行う
bear-bore-born 生む
left 左
nose 鼻
rule 治める

did nothing but cry
　　泣いてばかり
scold 叱る
kick out 追放する
father 父
climb 登る

older sister 姉
suspicious 疑う
think-thought 思う
take over 乗っ取る
wait 待つ
combat uniform 戦闘服

empire 皇室
ancestor 祖先
sun 太陽

第4章 スサノオ 大暴れ

スサノオは言いました、
「乗っ取る心はないです。清い心です。」
彼は提案しました。「清い心を示すために、
子どもを生みあいましょう。」
この提案は誓約と言います。
(「賭け」のことです。)
「誓約」の結果として、
アマテラスはの女の子を三人生みました。
スサノオは男の子を五人生みました。
どちらが勝ったのでしょう。
スサノオは宣言しました、「俺が勝った。」
そして彼は、天のあちこちで、
大暴れしました。

「スサノオ」は、「アマテラス」の弟です。

Chapter 4. *Susanoo* Violence

Susanoo said "I don't intend
to take over the heaven. I am pure".
He said, "Let's give birth to a child
to each other to show a pure mind".
This proposal is called *Ukei*.
(means Bet)
As a result of *UKEI*,
Amaterasu gave birth to three girls,
and *Susanoo* gave birth to five boys.
Which won?
Susanoo said "I won",
and he took violent actions
everywhere in the heaven.

Susanoo is a younger brother of *Amaterasu*.

Violence 大暴れ

intend ～するつもりである
take-over 乗っ取る
pure 清い
mind 心
proposal 提案

bet 賭け
result 結果
win-won 勝つ
declare 宣言する
violent actions 大暴れ
everywhere あちこちで

第5章 天岩戸 (あまのいわと)

岩戸(いわと)は、岩(いわ)の洞穴(ほらあな)で、
入口(いりぐち)に、岩(いわ)の戸(と)があります。

スサノオの大暴(おおあば)れが原因(げんいん)で、
アマテラスは岩戸(いわと)に閉(と)じこもりました。
世界(せかい)は真(ま)っ暗(くら)になりました、
なぜなら、太陽(たいよう)の神(かみ)アマテラスが、
岩戸(いわと)の中(なか)に隠(かく)れてしまったからです。
多(おお)くの神々(かみがみ)は、困(こま)ってしまいました。
それで、皆(みな)でどうするか相談(そうだん)しました。
アメノウズメが岩戸(いわと)の前(まえ)で、
面白(おもしろ)いダンスを踊(おど)りました。
それで、神々(かみがみ)が大声(おおごえ)で笑(わら)いました。

Chapter 5. *Amanoiwato*

Iwato is a rock cave and
has a rock door at the entrance.

Due to *Susanoo*'s violence,
Amaterasu hid herself in the *Iwato* cave.
The world had become very dark,
because the god of the sun, *Amaterasu*,
hid in the rock cave.
Many Gods were in trouble.
They discussed what to do.
So, *Amenouzume* danced humorously
in front of the rock cave.
All the gods laughed loudly.

rock 岩
cave 洞穴
rock door 岩の戸
entrance 入口

due to ～が原因で
hide-hid-hidden 隠れる
world 世界
very dark 真っ暗
because なぜなら

were in trouble 困った
discussed 相談
what to do どうするか
humorously ユーモラスに
laugh 笑う
loudly 大声で

「アメノウズメ」は、踊りの神様です。

Amenouzume is the god of dance.

Due to *Susanoo's* violence, *Amaterasu* hid herself in the *Iwato* cave.
The world had become very dark, because the god of the sun, *Amaterasu*, hid in the rock cave.

Many Gods were in trouble. They discussed what to do. So, *Amenouzume* danced humorously in front of the rock cave. All the gods laughed loudly.

第6章 岩戸開き

アマテラスは不思議に思いました。
「外は、どうして賑やかなのだろう？」
それで彼女は岩戸を少し開けました。
すると、隠れていたタヂカラオの神が、
岩戸を開け、アマテラスを、
外へ連れ出しました。

太陽の神が岩戸の外へ出られたので、
世界は、再び明るくなりました。
今回のトラブルの原因はスサノオでした。
神々は、スサノオのヒゲを抜きとり、
彼の手足の爪を全て剥ぎ取り、
彼を天から追放しました。

これで高天原神話を終わります。

「タヂカラオ」は、力自慢の神様です。

Chapter 6. *Iwato*' Open

Amaterasu said,
"Why is it so lively outside?".
So, she tried to open *Iwato* a little.
Then, the hidden god of *Tajikarao*
opened *Iwato* and took *Amaterasu* outside.

As the Sun god went out of *Iwato*,
the world became brighter again.
The cause of this trouble was *Susanoo*.
So, the gods pulled out his beard, and
peeled off his nails from his hands
and feet,
and expelled him out of the heaven.

This is the end of the *Takamanohara*
Mythology.

Tajikarao is the powerful god.

---

lively 賑やかに
outside 外は
hidden 隠れていた
outside 外

out of ～の外へ
brighter 明るく
cause 原因
trouble トラブル
pull out 抜き取る
beard ひげ
peel off 剥ぎ取る
hands and feet 手足
expel 追放する

powerful 力自慢の

Amaterasu said,
"Why is it so lively outside?".
So, she tried to open *Iwato* a little.
Then, the hidden god of *Tajikarao* opened *Iwato* and took *Amaterasu* outside.

As the Sun god went out of *Iwato*, the world became brighter again.

The cause of this trouble was *Susanoo*. So, the gods pulled out his beard, and peeled off his nails from his hands and feet, and expelled him out of the heaven.

Izumo

This is the end of the *Takamanohara* Mythology.

第二幕　出雲神話 / ACT II *Izumo* Mythology

第7章　八俣の大蛇 / Chapter 7. *Yamatanoorochi*

(means the eight headed giant snake)

eight headed　八つの頭の
giant　巨大な
snake　蛇

スサノオは天の高天原
から追放されました。
彼は天から出雲へ下ってきました。
そこで、彼は大蛇と戦いました。
その蛇は、恐ろしい怪物です、
娘たちを食べてしまうのです。
スサノオは蛇を退治しました。
それで、彼はクシナダ姫を助けました、
そして、彼女と結婚しました。

Susanoo was expelled
out of the heaven *Takamanohara*.
He came down from the heaven to *Izumo*.
He fought with the Giant Snake, there.
The Snake is a terrible monster
that eats daughters.
Susanoo defeated the Snake.
Then, he saved Princess *Kushinada*,
and married her.

expel　追放する
fight-fought　戦う
terrible　恐ろしい
monster　怪物

eat-ate-eaten　食べる
daughter　娘
defeat　退治する
marry　結婚する

「出雲」は、古い地名で、現在の「島根県」です。

Izumo is the old name, of current *Shimane* prefecture.

Susanoo was expelled out of the heaven *Takamanohara*. He came down from the heaven to *Izumo*.

He fought with the Giant Snake, there. The Snake is a terrible monster that eats daughters. *Susanoo* defeated the Snake. Then, he saved Princess *Kushinada*, and married her.

第8章 因幡の白兎

それから、長い長い年月が過ぎました。
大国主の時代になりました。
彼は、スサノオの六世の孫です。
あるとき、兎が裸にされ、泣いていました。
大国主は、兎を助けました。
しかし、その事件が元で、
彼は兄さんたちに、いじめられました。

Chapter 8. *Inaba's white Rabbit*

A long long time had passed since then.
The age of *Ohkuninushi* began.
He is the sixth generations grandson of *Susanoo*.
One day, a rabbit was naked and was crying.
Ohkuninushi saved the rabbit.
However, due to this incident,
he was bullied by his elder brothers.

rabbit 兎

pass 過ぎる
sixth-generations 6世の
grandson 孫

one day ある日
naked 裸にされ
cry 泣く
However しかし
due to ～が元で
incident 事件
bully いじめる
elder brothers 兄たち

「因幡」は、古い地名で、
現在の「鳥取県」です。
「大国主」は、「出雲」の神様です。

Inaba is the old place name, of current *Tottori* prefecture.
Ohkuninushi is the god of *Izumo*.

A long long time had passed since then.
The age of *Ohkuninushi* began. He is the sixth generations grandson of *Susanoo*.

One day, a rabbit was naked and was crying.
Ohkuninushi saved the rabbit. However, due to this incident, he was bullied by his elder brothers.

第9章 根の国の苦難

根の国は地下の根にある国です。

兄たちから身を守るため、
大国主は根の国へ
逃げてきました。
そこで、彼はスセリ姫と出会い、
仲良くなりました。
彼女はスサノオの娘です。
スサノオは様々な難題を
大国主へ与えました。
大国主は、蛇部屋や蜂部屋の中で、
彼女に助けられました。
彼は火攻めのときに、
鼠にも助けられました。
こうして、彼は様々な苦難を、
乗り越えました。
最後に、彼は彼女を連れ、根の国を、
脱け出すことに成功しました。

Chapter 9. *Nenokuni*'s hardship

Nenokuni is the underground country.

In order to protect himself
from his brothers, *Ohkuninushi*
ran away to *Nenokuni*.
There, he met Princess *Suseri*
and became friends with her.
She is the daughter of *Susanoo*.
Susanoo gave various difficult tasks
to *Ohkuninushi*.
Ohkuninushi was helped by her
in the snake room and the bee room.
He was also helped by a mouse,
in the fire attack.
In this way he overcame
various hardships.
At last, he took her and succeeded in
getting out of *Nenokuni*.

---

hardship 苦難

underground 地下

protect 身を守る
run-ran-run 走る
run away 逃げてくる
Princess 姫

became friends 仲良くなる
daughter 娘
various difficult tasks 様々な難題

snake 蛇
bee 蜂
mouse 鼠
fire attack 火攻め
overcome 乗り越える
hardship 苦難
at last ついに
succeed in 成功する
get out 逃げ出す

第10章 地上の王者

大国主は出雲へ戻りました。
そこで彼は、兄たちを打ち負かし、
地上の王者になりました。
アマテラスは、それを天で見ていました。
彼女は宣言しました、「地上の国は、
私の子孫が治めるべきである。」
それで彼女は使者を出雲へ送りました。
これは国譲りの交渉をするためです。

Chapter 10. The king of the land

Ohkuninushi returned to *Izumo*.
There, he beat his brothers, and
became the king of the land.
Amaterasu was watching it in heaven.
She declared that the land
should be ruled by her descendants.
Then, she sent her messenger to *Izumo*.
This is a negotiation to obtain the country.

land 地上

beat 打ち負かす
declare 宣言する
rule 治める

descendant 子孫
messenger 使者
negotiation 交渉
obtain 手に入れる

Ohkuninushi returned to *Izumo*. There, he beat his brothers, and became the king of the land.

Amaterasu was watching it in heaven. She declared that the land should be ruled by her descendants.

Then, she sent her messenger to *Izumo*. This is a negotiation to obtain the country.

Izumo

第11章 国譲り

Chapter 11. Handing over the country

hand over 譲る

3番目の使者として、タケミカヅチが地上に降りてきました。
彼は、剣の神です。
彼は「国を譲れ」と大国主を脅しました。
大国主はタケミカヅチに、出雲大社を建設することを要求しました。
タケミカヅチは、それを承諾しました。
それで大国主は、国を譲ることを、最終的に承諾しました。
出雲大社は、大きな神社です、出雲に、今も存在します。

これで、出雲神話を終わります。

As the third messenger, *Takemikazuchi* came down from heaven to the land.
He is the God of the Swords.
He threatened *Ohkuninushi* to hand over the country.
Ohkuninushi required *Takemikazuchi* to construct *Izumotaisha*.
Takemikazuchi accepted it.
Finally, *Ohkuninushi* accepted, the offer to hand over the country.
Izumotaisha is a large shrine in *Izumo*, which still exists.

This concludes *Izumo* mythology.

sword 剣
threaten 脅す
require 要求する

construct 建設する
accept 受け入れる
offer 要求

shrine 神社
exist 存在する
conclude ～を終わる

As the third messenger, *Takemikazuchi* came down from heaven to the land. He is the God of the Swords. He threatened *Ohkuninushi* to hand over the country.
Ohkuninushi required *Takemikazuchi* to construct *Izumotaisha*. *Takemikazuchi* accepted it. Finally, *Ohkuninushi* accepted, the offer to hand over the country. *Izumotaisha* is a large shrine in *Izumo*, which still exists.

This concludes *Izumo* mythology.

第三幕　日向神話

第12章　天孫降臨

アマテラスは、国を譲られて、
大変、喜びました。
そして彼女は孫のニニギを
高千穂の峰に降らせました。
ニニギは、コノハナサクヤ姫と
地上で出会い、結婚しました。
彼女は山の神である、大山積神
の娘です。

「ひむか」は、古い地名で、
現在の「宮崎県」です。
「高千穂の峰」は、
「ひむか」にある、山の名前です。
「高千穂の峰」は、二説あります。
一つは霧島の高千穂の峰、
今一つは高千穂町の二上の峰
「ニニギ」が地上へ降りたことを
日本語で、「天孫降臨」と呼びます。
日本語の「テンソン」は、
「アマテラスの孫」を意味します。

ACT III *Himuka* Mythology

Chapter 12. *Tenson*'s Advent

advent 降臨、到来

Amaterasu was very pleased,
that the country was handed over.
And she ordered her grandson, *Ninigi*
to descend to *Takachihonomine*.
Ninigi met Princess *Konohanasakuya*
on the ground and married her.
She is the daughter of *Ohyamatsuminokami*,
the God of Mountains.

was pleased 喜んだ
hand over 譲る
order 命令する
descend 降りる

Himuka is the old place name, of
current *Miyazaki* prefecture.
Takachihonomine is the name of
the mountain in *Himuka*.
There are two theories about *Takachiho*.
One is *Takachiho* in *Kirishima*.
and the other is *Futagamiyama* in *Takachiho* Town
The fact that *Ninigi* has landed on the
ground is called *Tensonkohrin* in Japanese.
Tenson in Japanese means
Amaterasu's grandson.

theory 説
land 着陸する
grandson 孫

第13章　火中出産

コノハナは、ニニギに報告しました、
「あなたの子どもができました。」
「本当に、俺の子か？」と、
彼は聞き返しました。
彼女は宣言しました。
「私は、火の中で、子どもを
産んで見せます。」
「もし赤ん坊が、あなたの子なら、
火の中でも、
無事に生まれるでしょう。
なぜなら、神様の子ですから。」
結局、
三人の子どもが、無事に生まれました。

Chapter 13. Childbirth in the fire

childbirth 出産
fire 火

Konohana said to *Ninigi*,
"I am expecting your child".
Then, he asked,
"Is it truly my baby?".
She declared.
"I will give birth to a child
in the fire."
"If the baby is yours,
it will be born safely
in the fire,
because it is the child of a god."
In the end,
three children were born safely.

am expecting 身ごもる
truly 本当に
declare 宣言する
give birth 産む

safely 無事に
In the end 結局
bear-bore-born 産む

Konohana said to Ninigi,
"I am expecting your child".
Then, he asked,
"Is it truly my baby?".

She declared.
"I will give birth to a child
in the fire."
"If the baby is yours,
it will be born safely
in the fire,
because it is the child of a god."
In the end,
three children were born safely.

第14章　海幸と山幸

火の中で生まれた子どもたちは
大人になりました。
兄のホデリは海で働きました。
それで、彼は海幸と呼ばれました。
（海の男の意味です。）
弟のホオリは山で働きました。
それで彼は山幸と呼ばれました。
（山の男の意味です。）
あるとき、彼らはお互いに道具を交換し、
別の仕事をしてみました。
しかし山幸は釣り針を失くし、
魚に取られてしまいました。
それは、兄の海幸が大事に
していた釣り針でした。

Chapter 14. *Umisachi & Yamasachi*

The children born in the fire
became adults.
The older brother *Hoderi* worked in the sea.
So, he was called *Umisachi*
(means Sea's man)
The younger brother *Hoori* worked
in the mountains.
So, he was called *Yamasachi*.
(means Mountain's man)
One day, they exchanged their tools
with each other, and tried different jobs.
However, *Yamasachi* lost the fishing hook,
because it was taken by the fish.
It was the fishing hook that was cherished
by his older brother *Umisachi*.

adult 大人

one day あるとき
exchange 交換する
each other お互いに
try 試す
different 別の
fishing hook 釣り針
take-took-taken 取る
cherish 大事にする

The children born in the fire became adults.
The older brother *Hoderi* worked in the sea.
So, he was called *Umisachi*. (means Sea's man)

One day, they exchanged their tools with each other, and tried different jobs. However, *Yamasachi* lost the fishing hook, because it was taken by the fish. It was the fishing hook that was cherished by his older brother *Umisachi*.

The younger brother *Hoori* worked in the mountains.
So, he was called *Yamasachi*.
(means Mountain's man)

第15章 海の宮

山幸は、釣り針を失くしたために
兄に強く、叱られました。
それで、彼は、青島の海岸を、
とぼとぼと歩いていました。

そこへ塩つちの神が現れました。
彼は「海の宮へ行きなさい」と教えました。
それで、山幸は、海の宮へ辿り着きました。
そこで彼はトヨタマ姫と出会いました。
彼女は海の神の娘でした。
彼は彼女と結婚しました。

「青島」は、地名で、宮崎市にあります。
「青島」は、橋で繋がっている島です。
「塩つちの神」は、潮の流れを司る神です。

Chapter 15. The palace under the sea

palace 宮

Yamasachi was strongly scolded
by his brother,
because he lost the fishing hook.
So, he trudged along the *Aoshima* coast.

scold 叱る
fishimg hook 釣り針
trudge トボトボ歩く
coast 海岸

There, God *Shiotsuchi* appeared.
He told "Go to the Sea palace".
So, *Yamasachi* arrived at the Sea palace.
He met Princess *Toyotama* there.
She was the daughter of the Sea God.
He married her.

appeare 現れる
arrive 着く
daughter 娘

Aoshima is a place in *Miyazaki* City.
Aoshima is an island, connected by a bridge.
God *Shiotsuchi* is the god who controls the tide.

island 島
connect つなぐ
tide 潮の流れ

第16章 釣り針発見

3年後のある日、
山幸は失くした釣り針を見つけました。
彼は釣り針を持って、地上の青島へ
戻りました。
そこで、彼は攻めてきた兄と
戦いました。
彼は、魔法の玉で、
兄をやっつけました。
そして、彼は兄を家来にしました。
それで、彼は2代目の後継者となりました。
その後、トヨタマは身ごもりました。

Chapter 16. Discovery of the fishing hook

discovery 発見

Three years later, one day,
Yamasachi found the lost hook.
He took it and returned to
Aoshima on the ground.
There, he fought with his brother
who had attacked him.
He defeated his brother
with the magic balls.
And he made his brother his servant.
And so, he became the second successor
of Ninigi.
After that, Toyotama became pregnant.

later 後（のち）
find-found 見つける
return 戻る

fight-fought 戦う
attack 攻める
defeat 打ち破る
magic 魔法

servant 家来
successor 後継者
pregnant 身ごもる

第17章 代わりの子育て

トヨタマは、ヤマサチに頼みました。
「私は、元の姿で、子どもを産みます。
だから、私の姿を、見ないでください。」
しかし、彼は、見てしまいました。
彼女は、サメの姿で、
子どもを産んでいました。
彼女の、元の姿を見られたので、
彼女は大変、恥ずかしく思いました。
それで、彼女は海へ帰ってしまいました。
代わりに、彼女の妹の、
タマヨリ姫が、子どもを育てました。
子どもの名前はウガヤ・フキアエズです。

ウガヤは、鵜の羽、を言います。
フキアエズは、屋根が葺き上がる前、を言います。
つまり、鵜の羽で屋根が葺き上がる前に、
生まれた子なので、このように
名付けられました。

Chapter 17. Surrogate child-raising

Toyotama requested *Yamasachi*.
"I will give birth in my original form.
So, please don't look at my form".
But, he saw her form.
She delivered the child
in the form of a shark.
She was embarrassed because
her original form was seen.
So, she returned to the sea.
Instead of *Toyotama*, her younger sister,
Princess *Tamayori* raised her child.
The child's name was *Ugayafukiaezu*.

Ugaya means cormorant's feathers.
Fukiaezu means before roofing.
He was given that name because
he was born before roofing
with the cormorant's feathers.

---

surrogate 代わりの
child-raising 子育て
request 頼む
original 元の
form 姿

deliver 産む
shark サメ、鮫
was embarrassed
　　　恥ずかしく思う
instead 代わりに
raise 育てる

roof 屋根を葺く
cormorant 鵜
feathers 羽

Toyotama requested *Yamasachi*.
"I will give birth in my original form.
So, please don't look at my form".
But, he saw her form.
She delivered the child
in the form of a shark.

She was embarrassed because
her original form was seen.
So, she returned to the sea.
Instead of *Toyotama*, her younger sister,
Princess *Tamayori* raised her child.
The child's name was *Ugayafukiaezu*.

第18章　ウガヤの家族

ウガヤが3代目となりました。
彼が大人になったとき、
彼は、タマヨリ姫と結婚しました。
彼女は、彼を育てた人です。
彼女は、彼の母の妹です、
すなわち、叔母さんです。
その後、彼らは、4人の子どもを持ちました。

これで、ヒムカ神話を終わります。
これで、神話を終わりますが、
あと一つの物語を
お話ししましょう。
神武東征を。

Chapter 18. *Ugaya's Family*

Ugaya became the third successor.
When he became an adult,
he married Princess *Tamayori*.
She was the person who raised him.
She was his mother's younger sister,
that is, an aunt.
After that, they had four children.

This concludes the *Himuka* mythology.
This is the end of this mythology,
But I will tell you,
one more story about
the *Jinmu-Tohsei*.
(means *Jinmu*'s Eastern country Conquest)

family 家族

successor 後継者
Princess 姫
raise 育てる
aunt 叔母

conclude ～を終わる
eastern 東方の
conquest 征伐

第四幕　神武東征
ACT IV *Jinmu's Eastern country Conquest*

conquest 征伐

第19章　高千穂の宮
Chapter 19. *Takachiho's Palace*

ウガヤの息子のうち、
4男の名前は、ワカミケヌです。
彼が後に神武と呼ばれる人です。
彼が高千穂の宮に
いるときのことです。
彼は決意しました、
「このヒムカは西過ぎる。
ヤマトは、東にあり、中心でもある。
ヤマトへ行こう。」
これを「神武東征」と言います。

Of *Ugaya*'s children, the name
of the fourth son is *Wakamikenu*.
He is a person later called *Jinmu*.
It was when he was
at *Takachiho*'s Palace.
He decided
"This *Himuka* is too west.
Yamato is in the east and also in the center.
 Let's go to *Yamato*".
This is called *Jinmu*'s Eastern country Conquest.

palace 宮
later 後に
decide 決意する

「高千穂」は、地名で、
現在の、おそらくは、宮崎市にあります。
「大和」は、古い地名で、
現在の「奈良県」です。
「神武天皇」は、最初の天皇の名前です。

Takachiho is a place,
perhaps in current *Miyazaki* City.
Yamato is the old name,
of current *Nara* prefecture.
Jinmu Tennoh is the name of the first emperor.

第20章　瀬戸内海を東進

神武は、ヒムカの美々津港を、
お舟出しました。

彼は、瀬戸内海を通り、
大阪の浪速に着きました。
しかし、彼は、そこでトミの軍勢に
負けてしまいました。
負けたのは、太陽を正面にして
戦ったからです。
それで、彼は紀伊半島を、
迂回することにしました。

「美々津」は、地名で、宮崎県にあります。
「瀬戸内海」は、地名です。
「浪速」は、地名で、大阪府にあります。
「トミ」は、人名です。(「トミのナガスネヒコ」の略称)
「紀伊」は、地名で、和歌山県にあります。

Chapter 20. The sailing east through *Seto* inland Sea

Jinmu left the *Mimitsu* port in *Himuka*.

He passed through the *Seto* Inland Sea
and arrived at *Naniwa* in *Osaka*.
However, he was defeated by
Tomi's army there.
He lost because he fought
facing the sun.
So, he decided to bypass
the *Kii* Peninsula.

sailing east through 東進
Seto inland Sea 瀬戸内海
leave-left 出発する
pass 通過する
be defeated 負ける
army 軍勢
fight-fought 戦う
facing ～を正面にして
bypass 迂回する
peninsula 半島

Mimitsu is a land, in *Miyazaki* prefecture.
Seto Inland Sea is a name.
Naniwa is a land, in *Ohsaka* prefecture.
Tomi is a person's name.
(omitted *Tominonagasunehiko*)
Kii is a land, in *Wakayama* prefecture.

omitted 略した

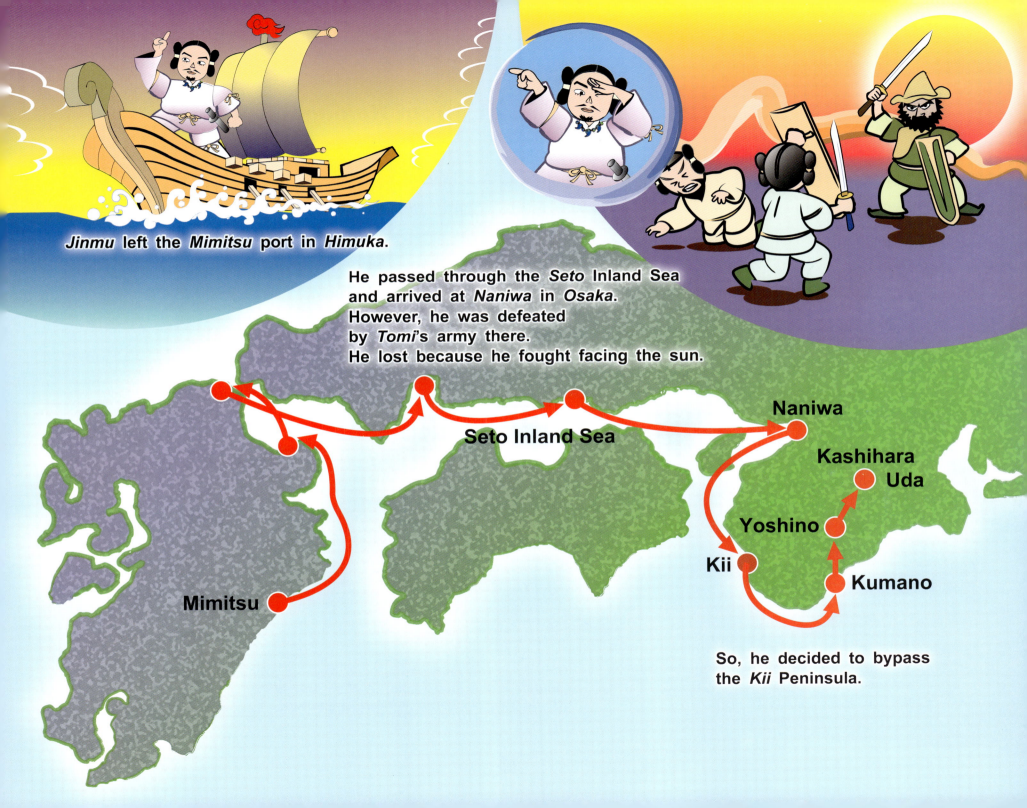

第21章 熊野から大和へ

神武一行は、熊野で再び上陸しました。
三本足のカラスが険しい山道を
案内しました。
三本足のカラスの名前はヤタガラスで、
案内の神様です。
そのお蔭で、神武一行は、
吉野の険しい山道を、迷うことなく、
越えることができました。
そして彼らは、大和の東の宇陀に
到着できました。
目指す大和は、あとほんの少しです。

「熊野」は、地名で、和歌山県にあります。
「吉野」は、地名で、奈良県にあります。
「宇陀」は、地名で、奈良県にあります。

Chapter 21. from *Kumano* to *Yamato*

Jinmu's group landed again in *Kumano*.
The three legged crow guided
them through a steep mountain path.
The name of the three legged crow
is *Yatagarasu*, the God of Guide.
Thanks to his help, *Jinmu*'s group was able
to cross *Yoshino*'s steep mountain path,
without getting lost.
And they were able to get to *Uda*
in the east of *Yamato*.
The target *Yamato* is just around the corner.

land 上陸する
leg 足
crow 烏（カラス）
steep 険しい

thanks to 〜のお蔭で
steep 険しい
get lost 道に迷う
target 目指す
around the corner
　　　　　あと少し

Kumano is the land name, in *Wakayama* prefecture.
Yoshino is the land name, in *Nara* prefecture.
Uda is the land name, in *Nara* prefecture.

Jinmu's group landed again in *Kumano*.
The three legged crow guided them through a steep mountain path.
The name of the three legged crow is *Yatagarasu*, the God of Guide.

Thanks to his help, *Jinmu*'s group was able to cross *Yoshino*'s steep mountain path, without getting lost.
And they were able to get to *Uda* in the east of *Yamato*.
The target *Yamato* is just around the corner.

第22章 初代天皇 / Chapter 22. The First Emperor

emperor 天皇

神武一行は、行軍の途中、
幾多の困難を乗り越えました。
彼らは、最後に、トミの軍勢と
再戦し、勝利しました。

The *Jinmu* group overcame many difficulties during the march.
They finally re-matched *Tomi*'s army, and defeated it.

overcome 乗り越える
march 行軍
difficulty 困難
defeat 打ち負かす
fight-fought 戦う

なぜなら太陽を背にして
戦ったからです。
そして遂に、彼らは、目指す大和の中の
橿原に着きました。
そして、神武は、初代天皇として、
即位しました。

This was because they fought with the sun at their back.
Finally, they arrived at *Kashihara* in their target of *Yamato*.
Then, *Jinmu* took the throne as the First Emperor.

throne 即位

これで、日本神話と神武東征を含む
全4幕を終わります。

This concludes all four Acts, including "Japanese Mythology" and *Jinmu Tohsei*.

conclude 〜を終わる
act 幕
include 〜を含む

ご清聴、ありがとうございました。

Thank you for your attention!

attention ご清聴

「橿原」は、地名で、「奈良県」にあります。

Kashihara is the land name, in Nara prefecture.

The *Jinmu* group overcame many difficulties during the march. They finally re-matched *Tomi*'s army, and defeated it. This was because they fought with the sun at their back.

Finally, they arrived at *Kashihara* in their target of *Yamato*. Then, *Jinmu* took the throne as the First Emperor.

This concludes all four Acts, including "Japanese Mythology" and *Jinmu Tohsei*.

Thank you for your attention !

October 9, 2021year, Works performed at National Cultural Festival In Miyazaki

Jinmu-Sama ~ The bond of life from God to Man ~

(Opening ~ Recolection of *Jinmu*)

    (writing)(the parentheses represent writing)
    (In the dark, chairperson introduces.
    Narrator and music band sit down.
    Music (wind-chime, shinobue)
    Light gets gradually brighter
    Children run around the stage.)

narrator Trampling the earth of ancient *Himuka*,
a boy run around like the wind.
His name is *Wakamikenu*.
    (*Jinmu* appears.)
    (*Wakamikenu* helps *Jinmu* to go up the stairs.)

narrator This boy *Wakamikenu* is *KamuYamatoiwarehiko*, that is, Japanese First *Tennou*, *Jinmusama*.
    (Children stop playing, and leave.)

Jinmu How beatiful *Mt.Takachiho* is!
Has it been shining in the same shape from the age of *Amaterasu*?
    (*Jinmu* leaves.)

narrator *Amaterasuohmikamisama* is the god of *Tennou*'s Family.
She bestowed three kinds of sacred treasures.
They have been handed down through the generations of the *Tennou*'s Family.

2021年10月9日　国民文化祭宮崎　での上演作品

「神武様──神から人への命の絆──」

（序　幕　　～神武の回想）

　　　　（ト書き）（カッコの中はト書きを表わす）
　　　　（暗い中、司会が紹介。
　　　　語りや音楽隊が着席。
　　　　音楽（ウインドチャイム、篠笛）
　　　　照明、徐々に明るく。
　　　　子どもたちが舞台を走り回る。）

語　り　太古のヒムカの大地を踏みしめ、
風のように走り回った少年。
その子の名はワカミケヌと申します。
　　　（神武　登場）
　　　（ワカミケヌは神武を段に上げる手伝いをする。）

語　り　この少年ワカミケヌこそ、カムヤマトイワレヒコ、
すなわち、日本の初代天皇神武様でございます。
　　　（子どもたちは遊びをやめ、退場する。）

神　武　高千穂の峰の何と美しいことか！
アマテラス様の御代から
変わらぬ姿で輝いているのだろうか？
　　　（神武　退場）

語　り　アマテラスオオミカミ様は、今でも天皇家に伝わる、
三種の神器を、お授けになった神様です。

- work　作品
- performe　上演する
- bond　絆
- recolection　回想
- parenthesis　丸かっこ
- trample　踏みしめる
- ancient　太古の
- shine　輝く
- shape　形
- bestow　授ける
- sacred　神聖な
- treasure　宝物
- hand down　後世に伝える

(ACT I　　Takamanohara Mythology)	**（第一幕　　高天原神話）**	performe　上演する
		universe　宇宙
(Slide projection starts.)	（スライド投影開始）	heaven　天
(Performers appear in order, and sit down.)	（出演者が順に登場、着席）	one after another
		次々と
narrator　There was nothing at the beginnig of the universe.	語り　はじめ、宇宙は、何もなかったのです。	land　国土
Soon, heaven and land were created.	やがて、天と地が創られました、	
And, *Amenominakanushi*, the God in heaven, appeared.	天に、アメノミナカヌシノカミが現れました。	
Then, many Gods appeared, one after another, the God" of men, *Izanaki*, and the God of women, *Izanami*, created the land of Japan.	それから次々と神様が現れ、男の神イザナキと、女の神イザナミのお二人が国生みをしました。	
(*Izanaki*, *Izanami* appear)	（イザナキ、イザナミ登場）	
duet　(*Kuniumi* in melody of *Ainosanka* (song of love))	デュエット　「国生み」（「愛の讃歌」のメロディで）	
man　What kind of body do you have?	男　そなたのその体、どんな体かな	
woman　My body is not completed. I have an unfinished part.	女　私の体は、成りなりて、成りあわぬ所、ひと所あり　成りあわぬ所、ひと所あり	
man　My body has an overly finished part.	男　われの体は、成りなりて、成り余る所、……成りなりて、成り余る所、ひと所あり	
I'll insert my overly finished part in your unfinished part, and, I'll give birth to the land of Japan. What do you think?	成り余るとこで、成りあわぬとこを、差し塞いで、国生みしようと思うのだが、これいかに？	
woman　It sounds great !	女　それはとても良いことですね	unfinished　未完の
two　Let's intertwine our fingers, while hugging,	男女　指をからませ、抱きしめながら、	intertwine　からませ
Let's drift in a dream world, and love each other,	夢の世界を、漂い、愛し合い、	drift　漂う
Let's give birth to the land of Japan, *Kuni-umi* !	二人で、日本を国生みしましょうね！	furthermore　さらに
narrator　In this way, the land of Japan was born. Furthermore, the tow gave birth to the gods who control nature, such as Seas, Rivers, Mountains, Trees, Grasses.	語り　こうして日本の国土が生まれました。さらに、海、川、山、木、草など、自然を司る神様を、次々とお生みになり、	
Finaly, The beautiful Japan is completed.	そして、遂に、美しい日本が、出来上がったのです。	

narrator	How many gods were born? Finally, when *Izanami* gave birth to the God of Fire, she died because of burns. So, she hid herself in the Land of the Dead *Yominokuni*. 　　(Lighting, getting darker) *Izanaki*, who mourned so much, chased *Izanami* to the land of the dead.	語　り	どれだけの神様がお生まれになったでしょう？ 最後に、イザナミ様が、火の神をお生みになったとき、火傷が元で亡くなられました。 それで黄泉の国へお隠れになったのです。 　　（照明、徐々に暗く） たいそう嘆き悲しまれたイザナキ様は、イザナミ様を、黄泉の国まで、 追ってゆかれたのです。

burn　火傷ヤケド
hide hid　隠れた
mourn　嘆く
frighten　おののく

	However, it is a dirty land. *Izanaki* was frightened by the transformed appearrance of *Izanami*. *Izanaki* escaped from the land of the dead in a hurry. So, they never met again. 　　(Lighting gets brighter.) *Izanaki* returned to the ground. In order to cleanse the dirty body polluted by the land of the dead, *Izanaki* played *Misogi*. At that time, *Amaterasu* was born from the left eye, *Tsukuyomi* from the right eye, *Susanoo* from the nose. From this *Amaterasu* to the first *Tennou*, *Jinmu*, Life is continuously connected.		しかし、そこは、穢れの地。 イザナミ様の、恐ろしく変わり果てた姿におびえたイザナキ様は、 急いで、黄泉の国を逃げ出しました。 そのため、二度とお二人はお会いすることがなくなりました。 　　（照明、明るくする） 地上に戻ったイザナキ様は、 黄泉の国で穢れた体を清めるため、 禊ぎをなさいます。 そのとき、左目からアマテラス、 右目からツクヨミ、 鼻からスサノオが生まれました。 このアマテラスから、初代天皇となるワカミケヌ様へ、連綿と、命が紡がれていくのです。

transformed
　　　　　　変わり果てた
escape　逃げる

cleanse　清める
polluted　汚された
continuously　連綿と

narrator	This *Misogi* chanted by the priest, remains in the *HaraeKotoba*, even today. Please listen！ 　　(Everyone stands up with a ratting sound.)	語　り	この禊ぎの事柄が、現代でも、神主さんが必ず唱える、「祓え詞」に残っています。 お聞きください。 　　（チャラチャラ音で、一同起立）

chant　唱える
priest　神主
remain　残る

Chorus	("*Harae-Kotoba*")	合 唱	(「祓え詞」)	
	Kakemakumo Kashikoki Izanagino Oukami		かけまくも かしこき 「イザナギ」の	
	Tsukushino Himukano Tachibanano Odono		おおかみ つくしの ひむかの	
	Awagiharani		たちばなの おどの あわぎはらに	
	Misogi harae Tamaishi Tokini		みそぎ はらえ たまいし	
	Narimaseru Haraedono Oukamitachi		ときに なりませる はらえどの	
			おおかみたち	
	Moromorono Magagoto Tsumi Kegare Arannoba		もろもろの まがごと つみ	
	Haraetamai Kiyometamaeto		けがれ あらんをば	
	Mousukotoo Kikoshimeseto		はらえたまい きよめたまえと	
	Kashikomi Kashikomimo Mousu		もうすことを きこしめせと	
			かしこみ かしこみも もうす	
	(Everyone sits doun with a ratting sound.)		(チャラチャラ音で、一同着席)	
narrator	We are very afraid!!	語 り	恐れ多くも、	afraid 恐れ多くも
	We would like to ask *Haraedono-oukami* born,		イザナキの大神が、筑紫の ヒムカの	would like to ask お願いしたい
	when *Izanaginooukami* conducted *Misogi*		橘の 小戸の 阿波岐原(のみそぎ池)で、	bear-bore-born 生まれた
	in *Tsukushi-o Himukano Tachibanano Odono*		禊ぎされたときに、生まれた	conducted …した
	Awagihara (in *Misogi* pond)		祓え戸の大神様に、お願いします。	
	Please exorcize various kinds of Evil, Sin,		私たちの心の中にある、いろいろな、禍、	exorcize 追い払う
	and Dirt in our heart. Please purify them!		罪、穢れをどうか 祓ってください！	various 様々な
	Please listen to what we ask!		どうか 清めてください！	evil 不幸、禍
	Respectfully, Respectfully, We will tell you!!		どうか お願いすることを 聞いてください！	sin 罪 dirt 穢れ
			謹んで 謹んで 申し上げます	purify 清める
				respectfully 謹んで
				legend 伝説
narrator	Let't start the famous *Amanoiwato* legend.	語 り	いよいよ、有名な天の岩戸伝説でございま	violent 暴れる
	Because the younger brother *Susanoo* is		す。	cave 洞穴
	too violent,		アマテラス様の弟のスサノオ様の、あまり	
	Amaterasu hid herself behind the door of		の乱暴ぶりに、	
	the rock cave.		アマテラス様は、岩戸にお隠れになってし	
	(*Susanoo* appears while playing the cynbal.)		まいました。	
	(*Amaterasu* appears while running around.)		(スサノオがシンバルを鳴ならしなが	

(Lighting, a little dark)
Because *Amaterasu*, the God of the Sun, hid herself,
The world has gone black.
The troubled Gods discuss with each other,
to lure *Amaterasu* from the rock cave.
Gods made *Amenouzume* dance.
  (*Amenouzume* appear while dancing)
  (Perfomers all cheer!)

Amaterasu
  Amenouzume!!
  Even though I'm not there, even though it should be black,
  Why is it so noisy outside?

Amenouzume
  Since the god who a noble than you appears,
  We are all happy and celebrating together.

narrator When *Amaterasu* peeks outside a little,
  Tajikarao took *Amaterasu* out of *Iwato* (rock cave)
  (Lighting on)
  And the world has regained light.

(Act II   *Izumo* Mythology)

narrator *Susanoo* was expelled out of *Takamanohara* and came down to *Izumo*.
  Then he defeated the *Yamatanoorochi* (giant snake), so he dominated *Izumo*.

ら登場、アマテラスは逃げる動作をしながら登場）
（照明は、少し暗く、）
太陽の神であるアマテラス様がお隠れになったので、
世の中は、真っ暗になってしまいました。
困った神々は相談し、アマテラスを誘い出すため、
アメノウズメに、舞を踊らせました。
　（アメノウズメ、踊りながら登場）
　（出演者全員が歓声）

アマテラス
　アメノウズメよ。
　私がいないのに、真っ暗なはずなのに、
　外は、どうして、そんなに、賑やかなのだ。

アメノウズメ
　貴方様よりも、高貴な神様が、お見えになったので、
　皆で、喜んで、お祝いしてます。

語り　アマテラス様が覗かれたとき、
　タヂカラオが、アマテラス様を岩戸の外へ連れ出しました。
　（照明点灯）
　そして、世の中は、光を取り戻しました。

（第二幕　　出雲神話）

語り　高天原を追放され、
　出雲へ下ったスサノオ様は、
　八岐大蛇を退治することで、
　出雲を支配する存在となりました。

---

lure　誘い出す、ルアー

even though　〜の筈なのに
noisy　賑やか
noble　高貴な
celebrate　祝う
peek　覗く
regain　取り戻す

expell　追放する
defeate　退治する
dominate　支配する

Then, a long long time has psssed.,
Ookuninushi of *Susanoo*'s Sixth grandson,
finally, became the King of Japan, after many trials.

There was a god who was watching the situation from heaven, *Takamanohara*. That god is *Amaterasu*.

Amaterasu
What a beautiful land!
This land should be ruled by my grandson, *Ninigi*.

narrator After several negotiations, *Ookuninushi* agreeded to *Kuniyuzuri* (the transfer of the land) to *Amaterasu*, on condition that she should build a fine shrine. This shrine is the current *Izumotaisha* shrine.

agreed 承諾する
transfer 譲る

(Act Ⅲ   *Himuka* Mythology)

narrator From *Takamanohara* to *Nakatsukuni*, *Niniginomikoto* desended from heaven. *Amaterasu* bestowed three sacred treasures to him as a proof of God.
(*Ninigi* bows and kneels)
(he receives treasures one by one)

Amaterasu
My grandson *Ninigi*!
I'm ready to leave!
Yasakanomagatama (ball)
and *Kagami* (mirror)

desend 降る
bestow 授ける
sacred 神聖な
treasure 宝物
proof 証
bow お辞儀をする
kneel 膝まづく
leave 出発する

それから、長い長い時がたち、
スサノオ様の、六世の孫の
大国主様は、数々の試練を経て、
遂に、日本の国の王となりました。

その様子を、天の高天原から、見ていたお方がいました。アマテラス様です。

天照　なんと美しい国だろう！
この国こそ、わが孫ニニギが治めるべきだ。

語り　幾度かの交渉ののち、大国主は、
立派なお宮を造ることを条件に、
アマテラス様への国譲りを承諾されました。
このお宮が、現在の出雲大社です。

（第三幕　ヒムカ神話）

語り　高天原から中つ国へ、ニニギ様は天下りました。
アマテラス様は、神の証しとして、
三種の神器を授けられました。
（ニニギは、お辞儀して、膝まづく）
（宝物を、一つ一つ受け取る）

天照　わが孫ニニギノミコトよ！
出発の準備は整った。
ヤサカの勾玉
そして鏡

	and *KusanaginoTsurugi* (sword) Bring all these down! The mirror is my soul! Think of the mirror as myself! And worship it! (*Ninigi* receives them one by one reverently, and bows deeply. The two leave.)
narrator	Thus, *Niniginomikoto* descended from heaven to the earth. (called *TensonKourin*) The party came down, with *Sarutahiko* as a guide at the top, squeezing and squeezing the clouds, slowly and solemnly.
narrator	*Niniginomikoto*, *Amaterasu*'s grandson, landed on the earth. He met a beautiful girl named *Konohanasakuyahime*. The two are attracted to each other, and had a one-night contact. Then time passed, and she was expecting a baby.
Konohana	Hi, *Ninigi*! Please rejoice! I'm expecting your baby!
Ninigi	Eh? Is it really my baby? I was with you only one-night.
Konohana	Dear oh! Do you doubt me? Then I'm prepared to give birth to a child in the fire!

	草なぎの剣 これらを、全て、持ち下れ！ 鏡はわが魂！ 我と思って、祀りなさい！ （ニニギは、一つ一つ、うやうやしく受け取り、深々とお辞儀する。二人とも退場）
語り	こうして、ニニギノミコト様は、天孫降臨されました。 一行は、案内役のサルタヒコを先頭に、雲を搔き分け、搔き分け、 ゆっくりと、厳かに、降りてまいりました。
語り	地上に降りたアマテラス様の孫のニニギノミコト様は、 美しい娘コノハナサクヤ姫と、出会われました。 お二人は、互いに惹かれあい、一夜の契りを交わされました。 それから間もなく、姫は子どもを身ごもりました。
コノハナ	ニニギ様!! お喜びください！ 私は、貴方様の御子を授かりました。
ニニギ	えっ?! 本当に私の子か？ お前とは、一晩だけだぞ。
コノハナ	まあ！ お疑いになるのですか？ それなら 私に覚悟があります。 私は、火の中で、子どもを産みます。

bring down 持ち下る
soul 魂
worship 祀る
reverently うやうやしく

squeezing 搔き分け
solemnly 厳かに

attract 惹かれあう
contact 契り接触
expecting a baby 身ごもる

rejoice 喜ぶ
doubt 疑う
prepared 覚悟する

narrator	After she declared it, she entered the maternity hut, and lit the hut. (The state of childbirth in the fire is expressed by lighting, acoustic, and dance.)	語り	姫は、こう宣言してから、 産屋に入り、産屋に火をつけました。 （火中出産の様子を、 照明、音響、ダンスで表現）	declare 宣言する maternity hut 産屋 express 表現する light lit lit 火をつける acoustic 音響 splendidly 見事に
narrator	Thus she splendidly gave birth to three children in the fire.	語り	こうして、姫は、見事に、火の中で、 三柱の子どもをお産みになりました。	
narrator	The brothers were born in the fire. The elder *Hoderinomikoto* called himself *Umisachihiko*. The younger *Hoorinomikoto* called himself *Yamasachihiko*. The location of this story is *Aoshima* (island). *Umisachi* hunts for fish in the sea, *Yamasachi* hunts for animals in the mountain.	語り	兄弟は、火の中で生まれた、 兄ホデリノミコトは海幸彦、 弟ホオリノミコトは山幸彦と名乗ります。 この話の場所は青島です。 海幸は、海の狩り、 山幸は、山の狩りをしました。	hunt for 〜を狩る lend 貸す fishing rod 釣竿
Yamasachi	Brother！ Please lend me your fishing rod！	山幸	兄さん！ 釣り竿を貸していただけないか！	
Umisachi	No！	海幸	ならぬ！	
Yamasachi	I want to hunt in the sea like you！	山幸	兄さんのように、海で狩りをしたいから！	
Umisachi	No！ Don't try unfamiliar things！	海幸	ならぬ！ 不慣れなことをするな！	
Yamasachi	Brother！ ・・・	山幸	兄さん！ ……	unfamiliar 不慣れな reluctantly しぶしぶ hook 釣り針、フック
Umisachi	・・・ Okay, Only this time！ (*Umisachi* reluctantly hands the fishing rod to *Yamasachi* and leaves to the right.) (*Yamasachi* goes fishing, and has his hook taken by a fish. (Stopmotion, blackout) (During the blackout, *Umisachi* appears	海幸	…… いいか、今回限りだぞ！ （海幸は、山幸に、しぶしぶ釣り竿を渡し、右側に去る。） （山幸は、釣りをする。そして、釣り針を魚に取られる。 （ストップモーション　暗転） （暗転の間に、海幸は右から登場し、左側の山幸と向かい合う。）	

from the right and faces *Yamasachi* on the left.)

(*Yamasachi* is hanging his head down.)

Umisachi Return my hook! No other hook is the same! No matter how many swords you crush, whether you make 500 or 1000, I will never receive them!

(Return the heels to each other, *Umisachi* leaves on his right.)
(*Yamasachi* slowly walks along the corridor on his left. The sound of the waves. Chorus start In the middle of the corridor *Toyotamahime* appears, the two stare at each other, and hold hands and leave to the left.)

Chorus (with the melody of *Hamabenouta* (The song of beach))
Yamasachi to look for the hook
Guided by *Shiotsuchinokami*
arrived at the *Watatsumi*'s palace
He married *ToyotamaHime*

narrator In the *Watatsumi*'s palace, The two were always together,
and wear living in peace.
One day, three years later, *Yamasachi* remembered the hook, and sighed
Watatsumi's god was worried, and discovered the hook.
And he handed *Yamasachi* the hook, two balls, *Shiomitsutama* and *Shiohitama*.

海　幸　（山幸は、うなだれている。）
私の釣り針を返せ！　同じものは一つとしてないのだ！
いくら刀を砕いて、五百作ろうが、千作ろうが、決して、受け取らぬ！
（互いに、きびすを返して、
海幸は、右へ。）
（山幸は、左の渡り廊下を、
ゆっくり歩く、
……波の音　　　……合唱、開始。
渡り廊下の途中で、トヨタマ姫が
現れ、二人は見つめ合い、
手を取り合って、去る。）

合　唱　（「浜辺の歌」のメロディで）
釣り針　　探しに　　山幸は
シオツチの神に　　導かれ
ワタツミの　宮へ　　辿り着き
トヨタマ姫と　　　結ばれる

語　り　ワタツミの　宮での、お二人は、片時も離れず、
仲睦まじく、暮らしておりました。
三年経ったある日、山幸彦様は釣り針のことを思い出され、ふっと溜息をつかれます。
心配されたワタツミの神は、釣り針を探してくれました。
そして、山幸彦様に、釣り針とともに、
潮満玉と潮干玉、丸い球二つを、渡されました。

hang his head　うなだれる
hook　釣り針、フック
no matter　たとえ〜でも
sword　刀
crush　砕く
whether　〜にせよ
heel　きびす、ヒール

corridor　廊下
stare　見つめ合う

sigh　溜息をつく
worry　心配する
discover　探し出す

Chorus	(with the melody of *Hamabenouta* (The song of beach)) *Shiomitsutama* and *Shiohitama* They control the waves of the sea. *Obochi, Susuchi, Majichi, Uruchi* Given the spirit of the curse. (At near the end of the song, appear from the right, *Umisachi*, from the left *Yamasachi*)	合 唱	（「浜辺の歌」のメロディで） 潮満玉と　潮干玉 ワタツミ　波を　司る オボチ　ススチ　マジチ　ウルチ 呪いの　言霊　授けられ （歌の終わりころ、 右から海幸、左から山幸、登場）

spirit 霊、ことだま
curse 呪い

Yamasachi	Brother! Sorry, I'm late! Finally, I have found your hook! (present the hook)	山　幸	兄さま！　遅くなって申し訳ありません！ ようやく、釣り針を見つけました。 　　（釣り針を差し出す）
Umisachi	What have you been doing? It's been three years! I won't receive it!	海　幸	何を今さら！ 三年だぞ！　受け取らぬ！
Yamasachi	Brother! ・・・	山　幸	兄さま！……
Umisachi	I don't need it anymore! (turn off the light a little)	海　幸	要らぬ！　（照明、少し落とす）

What have you been doing? 何を今更

Yamasachi	(in the tone of the incantation) This hook is *Obochi, Susuchi, Majichi, Uruchi*! (*Yamasachi* turns backwards, and with his hands behind his back, returned the hook.) (after a while, *Umisachi*, as if he was obsessed, receives the hook.) (Lighting, dimming)	山　幸	（呪文の調子で） このチは、オボチ、ススチ、マジチ、ウルチ！ 　　（山幸は、後ろ向きになって、 　　後ろ手で、釣り針を差し出す。） 　　（少し　間を置き、ウミサチは、取り 　　つかれたように、 　　釣り針を受け取る。）　（照明、暗転）

incantation まじない
backwards 後ろ向きに

obsess 取りつかれる
dim 薄暗くする
conflict 争い

narrator	By the incantation, *Umisachi*'s life has become worse. So, *Umisachi* attacked *Yamasachi* and it became a conflict.	語　り	呪いの言霊によって、 海幸彦の暮らしは追い詰められていきました。 そのため、海幸彦は、山幸彦に攻めかかり、 争いとなったのです。

	(Lighting, on) (*Umisachi* attack s *Yamasachi*, (During the next talk, the two are moving silently, *Shiomitsutama* is red, *Shiohitama* is blue.	（照明、ON）（海幸が山幸に襲いかかる （次の語りの間、二人は、動きのみ） （塩盈珠は赤玉、塩乾珠は青玉）
narrator	*Yamasachi* shakes *Shiomitsu* ball Big wave attacks *Umisachi*, and he sinks into the sea. "Help me！*Umisachi* cry！ Next *Yamasachi* shakes *Shiohi* ball, The water drains quickly, *Umisachi* emergs from the sea. *Umisachi* has survived, and has decided to serve *Yamasachi*. 　　（*Umisachi* leave to the right.）	語　り　山幸が、潮満玉を、振りかざします。 大波が海幸を襲い、海に沈んでいきます。 助けを乞う海幸。 次に、山幸が、潮干玉を、振りかざします。 すーっと水が引き、浮かび上がった、海彦。 生き延びた海幸は、山幸に仕えることになりました。 　　（海幸は、右へ去る。）

shake　振る
sink　沈む
drain　水が引く
emerge　現れる
survive　生き延びる
serve　仕える

narrator	After a while, *Toyotamahime* came to *Yamasachi* from *Watatsumi*'s palace. 　　（*Toyotamahime* rushed over along the corridor and hugged *Yamasachi*.）	語　り　その後、しばらくして、トヨタマ姫が、ワタツミの宮から、 山幸彦のもとにやってきました。 　　（豊玉姫が、渡り廊下より、駆け寄ってきて、山幸彦と、抱き合う。）
Toyotama	I have long wanted to meet you！ Please rejoice！ I am expecting your baby！	豊　玉　貴方様に、どれほど、会いたかったか！ お喜びください！　貴方様の御子を授かりました。
Yamasachi	How happy I am！Let's build a maternity hut in the cave of *Udo* immediately！	山　幸　なんと喜ばしい！ 早速、鵜戸の洞穴に、産屋を建てよう！
narrator	But, *Toyotamahime* went into labor, before the roof of the maternity hut is completed.	語　り　ところが、産屋の屋根が、葺き上がる前に、 豊玉姫は、産気づいてしまいます。
Toyotama	Please！ Never look into the way I give birth！ Never！ 　　（*Toyotamahime* leaves to the right. ）	豊　玉　お願いです！ 私の産む姿は、決して覗かないでください！　決して！ 　　（豊玉姫は、右へ去る。）

maternity hut　産屋
cave　洞穴
immediately　早速
go into labor　産気づく

	(*Yamasachi* leaves to the right a little later.)		（山幸彦も、少し遅れて去る。）	
narrator	But *Yamasachi* broke his promise,	語り	しかし、山幸彦は、約束を破って、	break-broke-broken 破る
	and looked into the maternity hut.		産屋を覗いてしまいます。	
	In the maternity hut, not his beloved wife		産屋の中には、愛しい妻ではなく、	terrifying 恐ろしい
	but the terrifying shark was fluttering around.		恐ろしいサメが、のたうち回っていました。	shark 鮫
Toyotama	(only voice)	豊玉	（声のみ）	fluttering のたうち回る
	Why didn't you keep your promise?		なぜ、約束を守ってくださらなかったのですか？	
	Embarrassed! Embarrassed! I can no longer live with you.		恥ずかしくて、恥ずかしくて、もはや、共には暮らせません！	embarased 恥ずかしい no longer 最早 entrust 託す
narrator	*Toyotama* entrusted *Yamasachi* with a newborn baby.	語り	豊玉姫は、生まれたばかりの子を、山幸彦に託して、	cry and cry 泣く泣く
	She cried and cried, and returned to her *Watatsumi* palace.		泣く泣く、ワタツミの宮へ、戻ってしまわれました。	
	(music)		（音楽）	
narrator	And, the wind across the sea carried *Toyotama*'s song.	語り	そして、海を渡る風が、豊玉姫の歌を、運んできました。	
	(*Toyotama* appears from the left,)		（豊玉姫が、左から登場、	
	(*Yamasachi* appears from the right.)		山幸が、右から登場。）	
Toyotama	(Solo singing) (with melody of *Yakumotatsu*)	豊玉	（独唱）（「八雲立つ」のメロディで）	
Song	Even the Red ball man has a glowing tail,		赤玉は　尾さえ　光れど	glowing 光る
	White ball, you dressed up, you are precious!		白玉の　君が装いし　尊くありけり	precious 尊い
narrator	(narative, at the No.2 of the song)	語り	（語りは、（「八雲立つ」のメロディで）	offshore 沖の
	A man like Red ball is fine		（2番）	sleep-slept 寝る
	but you like White ball" are even better!		赤玉のような男も、立派だが、	
			白玉のような貴方様は、もっと立派です。	
Yamasachi	(Solo singing) (at the No.3 of the song)	山幸	（独唱）（「八雲立つ」のメロディで）	
Song	Offshore bird, at the duck's island, I slept with you,		（3番）	
	I will never forget you! At everything in the world.		沖つ鳥　鴨どく島に　わが寝ねし	
			妹は忘れじ　世の事ごとに	
narrator	(narative, at the No.4 of the song)	語り	（語りは、（「八雲立つ」のメロディで）	
			（4番）	

Solo sing	I lived with you on the duck's island! I'll never forget beloved you in my heart! 　　(*Toyotama* to left, *Yamasachi* to right, leave) 　　(with melody of "Farewell song" 　　(Singer appear) Passed days, Autumu night, close our shoulders *Aoshima*, the moon floating in the wave, still the same I still love you after breaking up, to the moon Ducks! Tell my unchanging heart Where are you now? Ah-- Ah-- you　Ah-- you Where are you now? Call, but don't answer! Ah-- 　　(Singer leaves)	鴨住む島で　暮らしたね！ 愛した君を、いつまでも、心の中で忘れないよ！ （豊玉は左へ、山幸は右へ、退場） （独唱（「別れの曲」のメロディで） （歌手　登場） 過ぎし日　秋の夜　二人で　片寄せて 青島　波間に　漂う　月　今も同じ 別れた　貴方を　今でも　愛してると 月に　変わらぬ心を　伝えて　鴨たち 君　今　いずこか　あーー あー　君よ　あー　君よ 今　いずこ　呼べども　答えず あーー （歌手　退場）	farewell　別れの
narrator	*Ugayafukiaezu*, the baby left behind, was raised by *Tamayorihime*, the younger sister of *Toyotamahime* *Ugaya* grew up nicely, and married his foster parent, *Tamayorihime*, and was blessed with four boys. *Wakamikenu*, the youngest person of the four, is the one who will later become *Jinmu Tennou*. Thus three men, *Ninigi* → *Yamasachi* → *Ugaya*, are called *Himukasandai*, that is, *Himuka* three generations.	語り	残された赤ん坊のウガヤフキアエズは、 豊玉姫の妹、玉依姫に育てられました。 立派に成長されたウガヤは、 育ての親の玉依姫と結婚し、 四人の男の子に恵まれました。 そのうちのお一人、末のワカミケヌが、 後に、神武天皇となるお方なのです。 こうして、ニニギ → 山幸 → ウガヤと、 紡がれてきた、三人の命を、 ひむか三代と申します。	laeve（left）behind　残された raise　育てる grew　成長する nicely　立派に foster parent　育ての親 blessed　恵まれた

(Act IV　*Jinmutousei* (East-conquest) → return to the beginning)

	(*Jinmu* appear)
Jinmu	How beatiful Mt. *Takachiho* is!
	How it been shining in the same shape from the age of *Amaterasu*?
	(*Ithuse* appears)
	(The two sit face to face and talk to each other)
Jinmu	*Himuka*'s land is certainly beautiful.
	However, this land is too biased to the west to rule Japan.
	Brother! Would you like to go to *Yamato*?
Itsuse	That's right! I agree! Let's go to *Yamato*!
Jinmu	Let's go! To the east!
Itsuse	Now! To the east!　　(The two leave)
narrator	This is, so-called, *Jinmutousei* (East-conquest).
	Wakamikenu was married to *Ahiratsuhime*
	The two made an eternal farewell at *Mimitsu*.
	She sings a song of sadness.
	(*Ahiratsuhime* appears)
Solo sing	(with melody of Goodbye Galaxy Express 999 theme song)
	I was afraid this day would come
	This love won't reach you tomorrow
	I want to hold you in my heart, but
	It's a dream that won't come true, my love
	Goodbye set sail from *Mimitsu*
	Goodbye Don't look back and go

（第四幕　神武東征……序幕に戻る）

	（神武　登場）	
神武	高千穂の峰のなんと美しいことか！	
	アマテラス様の御代から変わらぬ姿で輝いているのだろうか？	
	（イツセ　登場	
	二人、向かい合って座り、話しかける。）	
神武	ヒムカの地は、確かに美しい！	certainly 確かに
	しかし、日本の地を収めるには、西に偏りすぎている。	bias 偏る
	どうだろう！　兄さん！　ヤマトへ行かないか！	
イツセ	そうだな。賛成だ。ヤマトへ行こう！	
神武	目指すは　いざ、東へ！	
イツセ	いざ、東へ！　　（二人　退場）	
語り	これが、いわゆる、神武東征です。	
	ワカミケヌは、吾平津姫と、結婚していましたが、	
	姫とは、美々津で、永遠の別れとなりました。	eternal 永遠の farewell 別れ sadness 悲しみの galaxy 銀河 theme テーマ afraid 怖かった
	吾平津姫は、悲しみの歌を歌います。	
	（吾平津姫　登場）	
独唱	（さよなら銀河鉄道999主題歌「さよなら」のメロディで）	
	この日が来るのが怖かった	
	この愛をあしたは届かない	
	貴方を胸に　抱いていたいけれど	
	かなわぬ夢ね　愛しい人	
	さようなら　お船出の美々津から	
	さようなら　振り向かず　行きなさい	

	You will now become stronger Go on a journey Goodbye (*Ahiratsuhime* leaves)		貴方は今　強くなって　旅立つの　さようなら （吾平津姫　退場）	journey　旅立ち
narrator	*Wakamikenu* left from *Mimitsu*, for *Usa*, *Tsukushi*, *Aki*, *Kibi*, ran the ship, to the east, arrived in the land of *Naniwa*, where battle with *Tominonagasunehiko* broke out. (the movement of the battle, Lighting blink, the sound of drums. Expression of battle.)	語り	ワカミケヌは、美々津を、お船出させ、 宇佐、筑紫、安芸、吉備と、 東へ、東へと、船を走らせ、 浪速の地へ着きました。 ここで、ヤマトのトミノナガスネヒコとの戦いになりました。 （戦いの動き、照明の点滅、 太鼓の音、などで、戦いを表現）	expression　表現 fight-fought　戦う lose-lost　負けた reflect　反省した travel　旅行した peninsule　半島
narrator	*Nagasunehiko* fought with the sun behind, and, *Wakamikenu* fought with the sun in front, so *Wakamikenu*'s army lost. "I was a child of the sun, but I lost because I fought against the sun." He reflected. So, traveled around the *Kii* peninsule and landed on *Kumano*. *Yatagarasu* took the lead, crossed the mountain, They arrived at *Uda*, east of *Yamato*. They fought against the army of *Nagasunehiko* again. (the movement of the battle, Lighting blink, the sound of drums. Expressin of battle.)	語り	ナガスネヒコは、太陽を背にし、 ワカミケヌは、太陽に向かって、戦ったので、ワカミケヌの軍勢は、負けてしまいました。 ワカミケヌは、「私は天つ神の子なのに、日に向かって戦ったから、負けたのだ」と反省し、 紀伊半島を回って、熊野から上陸しました。 熊野は険しい山。 ヤタガラスが先導し、山を越え、 ヤマトの東のウダに着き、 ヤマトにいる、トミのナガスネヒコの軍勢に再度、挑みかかりました。 （戦いの動き、照明の点滅、 太鼓の音などで、戦いを表現）	lead　先導 fight-fought　戦う victorious　勝利した exactly　正に
narrator	The sun was shining on the back of the victorious *Wakamikenu*, exactly the son of the sun. And, finally, he arrived at *Kashihara* of *Yamato*.	語り	勝利した、ワカミケヌの背後には、 まさに、日の御子、太陽が、 光り輝いていました。 そして、遂に、ヤマトの橿原へ到着されました。	

narrator	*Wakamikenu* called himself *Kamuyamatoiwarehiko*.		語り	ワカミケヌは、カムヤマトイワレヒコと名乗り、
	He came to the throne of the first *Tennou*, that is, *Jinmu Tennou*.	throne 王座 ascend the throne 王に就く region 領土		初代天皇、すなわち、神武天皇として、即位されました。
	(*Jinmu* appears with dignity)			（神武天皇が、威儀を正して、登場）
Jinmu	Now here, Japan, has become one country, I will ascend the throne as the first *Tennou*. From this land of *Yamato*'s *Kashihara*, Under heavens, the people of all four regions, Flatly, In peace, Under one roof, Like a family, I will continue to pray so that you can live.		神武	今ここに、日本は、一つの国となり、私は、初代天皇として、即位します。このヤマトの橿原の地より、天の下、四方の国の、諸々が、平らけく、安らけく 一つ屋根のもと、家族のように、暮らせるよう、祈り続けます。
Chorus	(with the melody of Song of Joy) The First *Tennou*! Our *Jinmu*! Praise for joy! Our *Jinmu*! Japan's Biginning! From this time! Born in *Miyazaki*! Our Pride!	pray 祈る praise 讃えよ pride 誇り	合唱	（「喜びの詩」のメロディで） 初代の天皇　　我らが神武 喜びたたえよ　我らが神武 日本の始まり　この時からよ 宮崎生まれが　我らの誇り
	(Everyone bows!)			（一同礼！）
	The end			完

この本は、下記の県内の多くの団体および多数の個人の方の協賛によりできました。ご協力を感謝いたします。

協賛団体一覧表

旭化成（株）延岡支社
（社会福祉法人）石井記念友愛社
岩切商事（株）
（株）永和産業
（株）エーコープみやざき
（株）NPK
エンジョイプラン
（有）ぎょうざの丸岡
（社会福祉法人）くすのき福祉会（おひさま保育園）
（株）国土開発コンサルタント
Salon Genbei　遊（佐々原）
三和ホーム宮崎（株）
（有）シンク
神話の杜みやざき
（有）菅自動車
（公益社団法人）生命保険ファイナンシャルアドバイザー協会
（株）ソラシドエア
東京海上日動火災保険（株）宮崎支店
トヨタL＆F宮崎（株）
（株）トヨタレンタリース宮崎
ニュースターコミュニケーション（株）
（医療法人伸和会）延岡共立病院
（株）ハンズマン
はますなPP総合事務所
（株）響
保険のアルプス都城支社
（株）マエムラ
（株）増田工務店
三井住友海上火災保険（株）宮崎支店
（株）南九州ファミリーマート
宮交ホールディング（株）
（株）宮崎魚市場

宮崎くみあいチキンフーズ（株）
宮崎県医師会
宮崎県建設業協会
宮崎県民共済生活協同組合
（公益社団法人）宮崎市観光協会
宮崎中央青果（株）
宮崎トヨタ自動車（株）
宮崎トヨペット（株）
（株）宮崎山形屋
（株）メモリード宮崎
米良電機産業（株）

青島神社
愛宕神社
天岩戸神社
荒立神社
今山八幡宮
潮嶽神社
鵜戸神宮
江田神社
大御神社
小戸神社
神柱宮
霧島岑神社
高千穂神社
都農神社
都萬神社
東霧島神社
早水神社
宮崎神宮
宮崎天満宮

この本を全ての学生に贈ります。
　　　（小学生、中学生、
　　　　高校生、大学生）

この本を、朗読や弁論大会や演劇などに
活用することを希望します。
できるなら、あなたがこの本を暗記
することを期待します。
もし、あなたが、この本を、暗記で話したら、
あなたは、尊敬されるでしょう。
外国の人は、日本の歴史の古さに
感心するでしょう。

I will give this book to all students
(of elementary schools, junior-highschools,
highschools, colleges and universities)

I hope this book will be used for reading,
speech-contests, stage-plays, etc.
If possible, I hope you can memorize
this book.
If you speak this book in memorization,
you will be respected,
Foreigners will be impressed,
by the oldness of Japanese history.

memorize　暗記する

memorisation　暗誦
respect　尊敬する
foreigner　外国人
be impressed　感心する
history　歴史

神様や場所の名前などは、斜体字で表した。
この本は、辞書なしで、やさしく読めるように、
できるだけやさしい文にした。

日本の神話 Japanese Mythology

「神話」の英語は、mythology、または myth である。
myth の方が、簡単であるが、女性の「〜さん」
（Miss）や「失敗」（miss）と紛らわしい。
それで、mythology を使うことにした。

The names of gods and places are written
in *italics*.
The sentences were made as easily as possible
so that this book can be read easily
without a dictionary.

italics　斜体字、
　　　　イタリック体

日本の神話
～日本語英語対訳～

2024年10月31日初版発行

日本語著者	・・・	湯川英男
		旭丘高、名大、トヨタ、神話の杜代表
英語翻訳者	・・・	髙橋明弘
		日南高、九大、県職員、英ケント大学院
英語監修	・・・	大竹克彦
		大宮高、鹿大、宮崎県高校教員
		元宮崎県立宮崎大宮高等学校英語教諭
絵	・・・	田畑吉親
DVD	・・・	飯牟禮真知子と仲間達
		宮崎国際大学 教授連
		ウォーカー ロイド、オチ デボラj、
		アダチ ジェイソン、シュミット レベッカj
発 行 者	・・・	神話の杜みやざき
		〒880-0841　宮崎市吉村町697番地6
		電話　090-1167-7581
発 行 所	・・・	（有限会社）鉱脈社
		〒880-8551　宮崎市田代町263番地
		電話　0985-25-1758
印　　刷	・・・	（有限会社）鉱脈社
協　　力	・・・	（公益社団法人）宮崎市観光協会
		（有）はにわ広告社
		宮崎県商工会議所連合会
		宮崎県神社庁

Japanese Mythology
～Japanese English Bilingual～

First edition issued, October 31, 2024

Author・・・Hideo Yukawa
　　　Asahigaoka(H),Nagoya(U),TOYOTA,Sinwanomori(Re)
English translator・・・Akihiro Takahashi
　　　Nichinan(H),Kyushu(U),Miyazaki(P),Kent(G)
Supervisor of English・・・Katsuhiko Ohtake
　　　Ohmiya(H),Kagoshima(U),Miyazaki(P)
　　　Former Miyazaki Prefectural Miyazaki Ohmiya
　　　High School English Teacher

Picture・・・Yoshichika Tabata
DVD　　・・・Machiko Iimure & her friends
　　　Miyazaki Intrrnational University Profesors
　　　Lloyd Walker, Debra j. Occhi,
　　　Jason Adachi. Rebecca J. Schmidt

Issuer・・・Shinwa-no-mori Miyazaki
　　　〒880-0841 Yoshimura-Town697-6, Miyazaki-City, Japan
　　　Telephone 090-1167-7581

Publisher・・・（LC）Koumyakusha
　　　〒880-8551 Tashiro-Town263, Miyazaki-City, Japan
　　　Telephone 0985-25-1758（main）

Printing・・・（LC）Koumyakusha

Sponsorship・・・
　（PIIA）Miyazaki City Tourism Association
　HANIWA Advertising Agency
　Miyazaki Camber of Commerce & Industry Federation
　Miyazaki Jinjacho